Parks After Dark

A BEGINNER'S GUIDE TO STARGAZING IN THE NATIONAL PARKS

by RICK SHAFFER

WESTERN NATIONAL PARKS ASSOCIATION

TUCSON, ARIZONA

Cover: Delicate Arch after the sun sets,
Arches National Park.

Left: The center of the glorious Milky Way
Galaxy rises above Southern Arizona's
Kofa Mountains.

OK, say it three times: "My day at the park isn't over when the Sun goes down!" The reason is that the "other half" of the sky comes alive at night under the dark skies we have in most of the national parks in the western United States. For example, did you know that if you look into that dark half of the sky you can see a galaxy more than 2 million light-years away with just your naked eye? Or that you can see craters on the Moon with just those binoculars your Aunt Tessie gave you for your birthday last year?

Well, you can see a LOT of our Universe with either your naked eye or with whatever binoculars you brought with you on your trip.

But you need a dark sky to see much of what's really interesting in the night sky. That's why I wrote this book: to provide a short, concise, inexpensive guide to the night sky in the western national parks. I want to get you hooked on astronomy as a lifelong avocation. But I have an ulterior motive. If you get hooked on astronomy, maybe you'll also join the effort to reduce the pollution of our dark skies with extraneous light. That's covered in the last few pages of this book.

So, What Can I See?

* * * * * * * * * * * * *

You likely made a trip to one of our national parks because of its natural beauty. It's fortunate, though, that many of our parks in the West are located where the night sky is fairly dark, so you can see the stars a lot better than you can see them back home.

It's tempting to try to tell you about the broad sweep of what you can see in a dark sky. But the goal here is to get you started, not to turn you into an astronomer overnight. So, I'll just tell you what you can see with just your naked eye and with binoculars. If you want to take the next step and find out what you can see with a small telescope, you'll find a list of resources at the back of the book that will help you do that.

In this book you'll find out how you can see the larger and brighter objects in the night sky. I've already mentioned the Moon, which is arguably the brightest object you can see at night, but there are many others. There are also phenomena within our own atmosphere that can only be seen well under a dark sky. Earth satellites orbit just above our atmosphere, and you can see many of them from a dark-sky location. You can see all the planets except Pluto with either your naked eye or binoculars. You can also see many asteroids, meteors, and comets. Most stars are double, and many of the brighter ones can be "split" in binoculars. There are also clusters of stars, and nebulas (clouds of gas and dust). Some nebulas are dark, and we only see them because of what they obscure. Finally, you can at least detect many galaxies with binoculars; most will be a little more than faint smudges.

A Sky Primer

• • • • • • • • • • • • • •

This book won't teach you astronomy in any great depth. Besides, you probably don't want to start doing any "heavy astronomy lifting" while you're on vacation. So, I'll just give you a brief run-down of what's out there for you to see.

Everything looks like it's the same distance away in the sky, because everything in the sky is so far away that our "binocular vision" doesn't sense any depth to the view. The early history of astronomy was taken up with finding out the size of the things we see in the sky and how they move. You can learn all about this in a good text on astronomy.

It makes sense to me to start with what's close, and work our way to the edge of the Universe. One sky phenomenon you can see during twilight is the Earth's shadow. To see it, all you need to do is look close to the horizon opposite where the Sun just set. A few minutes after sunset, you'll see a dark blue band begin to rise above the horizon. When you first see it, the band will be at its darkest. As it rises, it will fade, until it disappears into the dark sky near the end of twilight. The dark band marks the edge of the shadow of the Earth's horizon. Above the band, red light from the Sun is illuminating the atmosphere. The band looks blue because the blue portion of the sunlight has been scattered into the shadow by dust particles. If you can see the Earth's shadow vividly, there's little dust or humidity in the air.

Twilight deepens over prehistoric dwellings at Hovenweep National Monument along the Colorado-Utah border.

An image of the planet Mars taken by the Hubble Space Telescope

With one exception, everything you can see in the sky from the continental United States is within our own galaxy, the Milky Way. Our galaxy is a vast disk of stars, gas, and dust that's 80,000 to 100,000 light-years across. The dust blocks our view of the spiral arms, because we're right in the disk of the galaxy. And the gas clouds are where new stars are forming. The gas is mostly hydrogen. There are something like 100 billion stars in our galaxy. It's in the shape of a great spiral, similar to the Andromeda Galaxy shown in the picture on the next page. Our Sun lies 30,000 to 35,000 light-years from the center and takes about 200 million years to make one trip around the spiral. (I'll explain the light-year a little bit later on.)

Within our galaxy are more than 1,000 clusters of stars. Galactic clusters, also called open clusters, are groups of stars that all formed out of the same cloud of gas. These clusters are particularly easy to see with binoculars. The other variety of cluster, the globulars, are enormous ball-shaped aggregations that might have 100,000 to 1,000,000 stars. They're extremely old. Some of them appear to have stars at least as old as our galaxy. There are approximately 150 globular clusters arranged around the center of the disk of the Milky Way Galaxy. They're nice to look at with a telescope, but not so spectacular with binoculars.

Beyond our galaxy is a lot of empty space, and a lot more galaxies. Our galaxy is part of a group of galaxies called the *Local Group*. The flagship of this group is the Great Andromeda Galaxy, which is the only object not in our galaxy we can see with the naked eye. Many of the galaxies we can see with binoculars are part of the Local Group.

Beyond the Local Group are more clusters of galaxies, innumerable galaxies. In fact, it doesn't matter what size telescope we use, or in what direction we look, all we see are galaxies.

You probably learned in school that Earth satellites can be seen for a few hours after sunset and for the same period before sunrise. They're actually orbiting higher above the Earth than the meteors we see on most clear nights. (Meteors are 40 to 70 miles up, while satellites are at least 125 miles up.) In fact, some meteors we see are actually satellites that have lost enough energy due to friction with the upper atmosphere to be forced to re-enter. Meteors are generally moving a lot faster than satellites, 30 to 40 miles per second, while satellites move at only 5 miles per second. So, a bright, slow-moving meteor may be a satellite re-entering the atmosphere.

Our Moon orbits the Earth in about a month ("moonth"), and the Earth-Moon pair orbits the Sun in one year. Two planets, Mercury and Venus, orbit between Earth and the Sun, so they're never found very far from the Sun in the sky. Mars is just out from the Earth.

Just out from Mars is the asteroid belt, some of which you can see with binoculars. Past the belt lie the orbits of the "gas giants," Jupiter, Saturn, Uranus, and Neptune, planets that are mostly gas and liquid, with only small solid cores. Pluto is a tiny iceball out beyond all the others. The Solar System also has a belt of icy objects like Pluto called the Kuiper Belt. Pluto is likely the largest and closest of these objects. There's also a spherical cloud much farther out from the Sun than the Kuiper Belt. It's called the Oort Cloud, after the astronomer who inferred that it must be there. It's where most comets originate. These "dirty snowballs" are mostly ice, dust, and a bit of gravel. They're not very big until they pass close to the Sun. When the Sun warms the ice, it *sublimates* (changes from solid to gas without going through a liquid phase) into a cloud of gas and dust, creating an object bigger than anything other than the Sun!

Opposite page: A wide-angle shot of the sky taken by the author in March 1997, when comet Hale-Bopp was at its finest. At the left you can see a cone of light extending from the horizon to the Pleiades cluster. This cone of light is called the zodiacal light and is caused by dust in the plane of the Earth's orbit reflecting sunlight into the viewer's eye. The Hyades cluster is just above the Pleiades at the left edge of the picture. The red splotches are emission nebulas in the Milky Way.

Above: The double cluster in the constellation Perseus. Although open clusters are quite common, this pair is exceptional due to the large number of young bright stars in each and their closeness while still being clearly distinguished.

Right: M31, the Great Andromeda Galaxy, the "flagship" of the Local Group of galaxies. The lanes of dust between the regions where stars are forming are obvious, as are the two satellite galaxies. This object is a fine sight with binoculars from a dark location.

The Basics of Looking at the Sky

* * * * * * * * * * * *

You won't turn into an experienced sky observer overnight. Only time under the stars can gain you that. But there are a few basic principles that will help you understand what you're seeing in a dark sky. Here they are:

EVERYTHING'S MOVING It will take at least 15 minutes for your eyes to adapt to the dark. During that period, pick the brightest object you can see near one of the horizons. Notice its position relative to a tall tree, mountaintop, or some other landmark. As your eyes adapt, you should notice that the object is moving mostly up if you're looking east, mostly down if you're looking west, or mostly from left to right if you're looking south to view it. (If you're looking at the sky with your kids, make a game of looking away from the bright object for ten minutes, and see how much it's moved. If you're a kid and you've dragged your mom and dad out to look at the stars, have them do it!)

BRIGHTNESS We call how bright a star appears in the sky its *magnitude*. The 22 brightest stars are 1st magnitude or brighter. On average, stars of the 2nd magnitude are 2.5 times dimmer than those of the 1st magnitude, and so on down the line. On a moderately dark night, we can see stars that are of about the 5th magnitude. On dark nights, we can see 6th magnitude stars and on very dark nights, 7th magnitude. The table at the right gives you the number of stars you can see by magnitude.

How bright an object appears in the sky is governed by how bright it actually is and how far away it is from us. The brightest star in Earth's skies, Sirius, shines at magnitude 1.4, but its actual brightness is much less, because it's very close to us, only 8.2 light-years away. Finally, an object that's spread out, like a nebula or the tail of a comet, can have a total magnitude that's fairly bright, but not be very easy to see.

DISTANCE Space is so big that it's not really useful to measure distances in miles or kilometers. Instead, astronomers use units based on how far light travels in a unit of time. So, the Moon is about 240,000 miles away, but we normally say that it's $1\frac{1}{3}$ light-seconds distant. The Sun is 93,000,000 miles away, but we usually say that it's 500 light-seconds, or $8\frac{1}{3}$ light-minutes, away. When Jupiter is closest to us, it's 2100 light-seconds, or 35 light-minutes, away. (See the table on page 11 for a bit more on how far various objects are from Earth.)

We measure the distance to everything beyond the Solar System in light-years. The closest star to us, α Centauri, is about 4.3 light-years away. Besides being convenient, this system forces us to think about *now* and *then*. Now is only inside heads. Everything we see is already in the past, because the light it emits took some time to get to our eyes. Of course, *your now* is different from mine, because you're not in the same place I am. (Einstein folded this into his theory of relativity.) It might seem obvious, but it's important to realize that the farther we see into the Universe, the earlier in time we're viewing. So, we can see as far in light-years as the Universe is old. Astronomers have determined that the Universe is 13.8 billion years old, so we can't see any farther than 13.8 billion light-years, because the light from whatever's farther away than that hasn't had time to reach our eyes!

COLOR A star's color can tell you a lot about it. In general, the bluer a star is, the hotter it is, and the redder it is, the cooler it is. Two familiar stars in the constellation Orion illustrate this. Betelgeuse is an enormous cool star. We see it as orange or red. Rigel is an extremely hot star, and we see it as blue-white. Many folks don't see star colors easily with their naked eye, but the colors become a lot more obvious through binoculars. (And kids see star colors a lot better than adults.) As you continue to view the sky, you may find that you notice the colors of the stars better than when you began. Finally, some objects are the color they are because of light they reflect, like the Moon and planets, while others—some nebulas, for example—shine like fluorescent lights.

A visitor peruses the rising summer sky from the South Rim of the Grand Canyon. The Grand Canyon Star Party is held every June at both rims of the park.

Number of Stars Visible by Location

MAGNITUDE	# OF STARS	TOTAL VISIBLE*	LOCATION
1 or brighter	22	22	Large city center
2	71	93	Urban area
3	190	283	Close-in suburbs
4	610	893	Suburban
5	1,929	2,822	Fairly dark
6	5,946	8,768	Dark
7	23,765	32,533	Unpolluted

Of course we can see only half the sky at any one time, so you should mentally divide these numbers by two to know how many stars you can see at any one time.

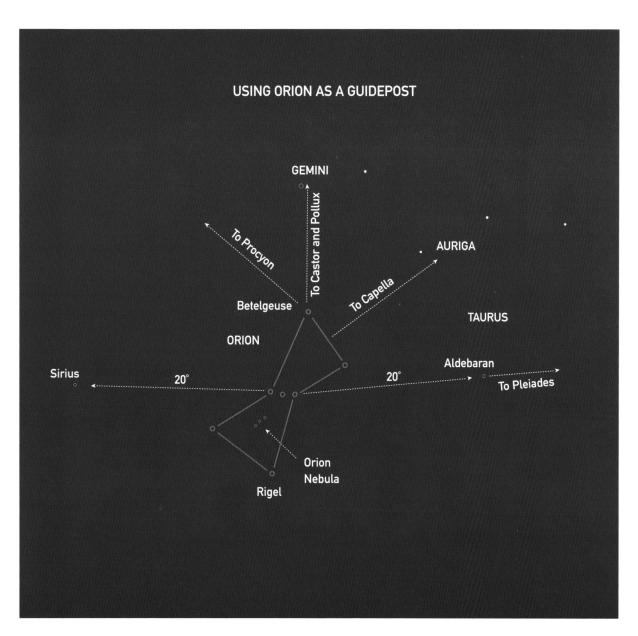

USING ORION AS A GUIDEPOST

GEMINI

To Procyon

To Castor and Pollux

AURIGA

Betelgeuse

To Capella

ORION

TAURUS

Aldebaran

Sirius · · · · · · · · 20° · · · · · · · · 20° · · · · · · · · To Pleiades

Orion
Nebula

Rigel

PUTTING IT TOGETHER We see everything in the night sky as if it's all painted onto a black sphere that's really far away. It's called the *celestial sphere*, and astronomers find positions on it in a very similar way to how we denote positions here on Earth. There's a *celestial equator*, which is just the Earth's equator projected onto the celestial sphere.

As I mentioned earlier, the objects that appear to move in the sky from night to night (or, in the case of meteors and satellites, a lot faster), are all here in our Solar System. The Sun appears to move along a line in the sky we call the *ecliptic*. It got its name because eclipses of the Sun and Moon are related to it. But, of course, the Sun appears to move once around the sky each year because the Earth orbits the Sun in that time. Since the nine planets all move in nearly the same plane as the Earth's orbit, they also appear to move through the sky very near the ecliptic. That's why the star maps include the ecliptic as the narrow yellow band.

Although modern astronomers don't make use of constellations to find objects in the sky, those of us who view the sky for pleasure still use them as handy memory aids to find our way. There are 88 recognized constellations that divide up the sky, some of which we never see here in the United States, because they're too far south. In fact, about 25 percent of the sky is invisible to us here in the northern hemisphere. Conversely, folks in a place as far south as Australia never see the northernmost 25 percent of the sky that we do.

Just as some southern constellations never rise above our horizon at all, others never set. These are called the *circumpolar constellations*, and they're in the sky even when the Sun's light blots them out. If you take a look at the six all-sky maps, you can see that the Little Dipper circles around the north celestial pole (NCP) as it moves around the sky from month to month. If you look at other constellations that are as close to the NCP as the Big Dipper, you'll see that they circle the NCP as well. You might be tempted to regard this as merely a curiosity, but the circumpolar stars serve as a convenient "anchor" for those parts of the sky that do rise and set. I've chosen to start my narrative for each of the maps with the brightest object on that map. But you should also look at the circumpolar stars, especially the "dippers" and the constellation Cassiopeia as a quick way to orient yourself in the sky. The chart on page 10 should also help you find the brightest stars.

The early constellations mostly represent the various gods and goddesses of ancient mythology. (Remember, this was before TV and video games, when folks had to take their amusement where they found it. You should also remember the myths were certainly the plots of the first "soap operas.") The later (southern) constellations represent mostly seafarers' and scientific tools. And, of course, the 12 constellations that lie along the ecliptic are the signs of the zodiac of the practice of astrology. (Astronomers don't recognize astrology as a science, but if you want to find your sign in the sky, I won't tell.)

Some of the constellation figures are fairly easy to recognize, and some are just plain "gapfillers." They do help us to find our way, so I've included them on the maps. And even if the stories do remind us of a bunch of "deities behaving badly," they are fun to find in the sky. They also help connect us to our past. If you're not impressed by this cultural justification for learning the constellations, just think of how you can impress your friends with your knowledge of the sky. Just don't assume that you'll actually be able to trace out a "reclining virgin" when you look at the constellation Virgo!

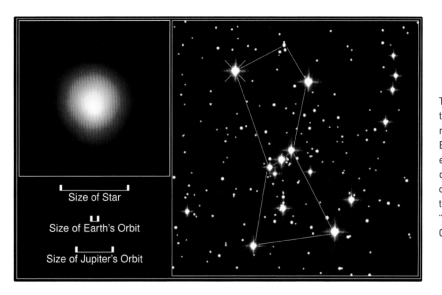

This diagram shows the size of the red giant star Betelgeuse relative to the orbits of the Earth and the planet Jupiter. It's easy to see why Betelgeuse is described as a giant. On the chart on page 10, Betelgeuse is the star at the upper left of the "box" that forms the body of Orion, the Hunter.

How Big/How Far?

OBJECT?	HOW BIG?	HOW FAR?	COMMENT
Meteors	Grain of sand	40-70 miles up	30-45 miles/sec
Earth satellite	10-100 feet	125 miles	speed: 7 miles/sec
Earth's Moon	2,160 miles	240,000 miles	$1^1/_3$ light-sec distant
Sun	880,000 miles	93,000,000 miles	Pretty hot….
Other planets	3,030-88,850 miles	10.4 light-year (ly) +	Big ones, small ones….
Asteroids	590 miles or smaller	Within orbit of Jupiter	One caused extinction of dinosaurs
Comets	Can be huge	Near miss of Earth to edge of Solar System	
Kuiper Belt	Asteroid size	Beyond Pluto	Icy objects
Oort Cloud	BIG!	$1^1/_3$ ly	Lotta comets
Nearest star	about size of Sun	4.3 ly	α Centauri
Milky Way Galaxy	80,000-100,000 ly	30,000 ly from center	We're in it
Andromeda Galaxy	125,000 ly	2.3 million ly	Queen of Local Group
Virgo Cluster	10 million ly	50 million ly	Closest cluster of galaxies
Closest super-clusters of galaxies		300 million ly	Several at this distance
Great wall of super-clusters		500 million ly	Largest structure in Universe
Observable Universe	27.6 billion ly	13.8 billion ly	May be bigger

Tools for Looking at the Sky

* * * * * * * * * * * * * *

THE BASIC TOOL, YOUR EYES You've likely noticed that your eyes take a while to adapt to the dark when you go out under the stars. That's because the iris in your eye takes a while to open up and let the maximum amount of light into the retina. The retina is the "sensor array" in your eye. It makes a chemical change in response to low light in order to become more sensitive.

Your retina actually has two zones of sensors. The *cones* are in the center, and they're good at resolving objects and revealing their color, but they're not very sensitive to low light. The *rods* are arrayed around the edge of your retina. They're sensitive to dim light, but don't resolve or show colors well. You can take advantage of the sensitivity of the rods in your eye by deliberately looking at large, faint objects off-center, or "out of the corner of your eye." You'll find that they'll brighten up. You can even do this with binoculars or when you look through a telescope.

You'll find that you can estimate the angular size of objects in the sky by using the various parts of your hand held at arm's length. (Don't try to hold your hand further than arm's length… Just kidding!) The long part of your clenched fist is about 10 degrees. You can prove this by counting how many "hands" it takes to go from horizon to *zenith* (top of the sky). It'll be about "nine hands," or 90 degrees. The width of three fingers is about 5 degrees across, and if you spread your hand, it will be almost 25 degrees across when seen at arm's length.

Using your hand to determine the angular size of an object in the sky is fairly easy. To find an object's position is a bit more difficult. There's a whole coordinate system—that's what you'd get if you "exploded" the longitude and latitude lines off the Earth and onto the celestial sphere. We won't be using that system. Instead, we'll use a system based on the horizon and the cardinal points: north, south, east, and west.

If you look at the horizon due north, you're at the starting point. The angular measure around the horizon, or parallel to it, is called *azimuth*. Due north is 0 degrees, due east is 90 degrees, due south, 180 degrees, and due west is 270 degrees. Once you go another 90 degrees from due west, you're at 360 degrees, which you can "reset" to 0. The angle above the horizon is called *altitude*. Since we must measure only from the horizon to the zenith, we need only 90 degrees to do it.

To just enjoy the sky using the maps in this book, you don't need to worry about azimuth and altitude. But if you want to find a satellite, knowing the azimuth and altitude is important. And if you see a really bright meteor, using your "10-degree fist" to estimate how far it traveled across the sky will give you more "sky credibility" than if you say something like, "it was *this* long," while holding your arms wide.

BEYOND YOUR NAKED EYE Even that pair of binoculars your Aunt Tessie bought you at "the discount store out on the highway" will show you much more of the sky than you'll see with just your eyes. For example, you

should be able to see many craters on the Moon and the four brightest satellites of Jupiter with a decent pair of binoculars. Also, you won't see the rings of Saturn, but you might see Titan, Saturn's largest and brightest moon. (You'll need a telescope to get a good view of the disks of the planets.)

If you have a pair of binoculars labeled "8x22" it means that the binoculars magnify eight times, and that the lenses at their "sky end" are 22 mm in diameter, a bit less than an inch. In general, binoculars more powerful than 8x are hard to hold while viewing the sky. Also, binoculars with small lenses don't give you as bright an image of faint objects as those with larger lenses. I recommend 7x50 binoculars to folks who ask me what to buy for looking at the sky. Generally binoculars that cost you less than about $100 won't be ideal for viewing the sky, but if you can't afford to spend much, any you can find will do.

If you can, mount your binoculars on a tripod to steady them. You can also steady them by holding them next to a tree or post. Finally, resting your elbows on the roof of a small car while holding the front of the binocs with your hands will steady them quite a bit. Just don't pick an unknown car in a parking lot. The alarm might be an unpleasant surprise!

The next step up would be buying a telescope. To make a bad joke, it's "beyond the scope of this book" to tell you what telescope to buy. There are other books that can help you with this, including one I wrote. Also, the members of your local astronomy club can help you with advice on buying a telescope.

You can use your fingers and fist held at arm's length to determine the angular size of an object on the sky.

The illustration at the bottom right shows the relative size of the planets from the smallest (Pluto) to the largest (Jupiter). The edge of the Sun is included for comparison.

The edge of the SUN

Pluto

Mercury

Mars

Venus

Earth

Neptune

Jupiter

Uranus

Saturn

Your First Night Out Under the Stars

* * * * * * * * * * * * * *

Getting to know the stars doesn't require much: some star maps, a flashlight, some items to keep you warm and comfy, and, of course, patience. Let's start with the maps. This book contains six *all-sky maps*. Each map is laid out to show you the sky as it will appear from places like Memphis and Albuquerque at about 9:20 PM local standard time on the dates you'll find listed next to each map. (Other dates and times are listed in the "fine print.") You'll also notice that the cardinal points are marked. So, if the text tells you to look east, you'll just put the point marked "E" down, and you'll see the stars that will appear near the eastern horizon.

To find out what direction is east, you'll need a compass or a map. Both work well. Or, if you remember where on the horizon the Sun set, you'll have a fair idea which direction is west. Just remember that the Sun sets north of due west in the summer and south of due west in the winter. In the spring and fall, the Sun sets very close to due west.

You'll need a flashlight to read the all-sky maps at night, but please don't use just any flashlight. You'll find that will ruin your night vision. Rather, use a red light. It works because our eyes won't "close down" in the presence of red light. You can get lights that have accessory red lenses, or you can buy a flashlight that uses a "red-LED" instead of a common bulb. The latter works better, but it is generally more expensive than the former.

Don't worry if you don't see everything I've described in the text for a particular map on the first night. Remember, there won't be a quiz at the end of the hour. Just find as many constellations or objects as you feel comfortable finding. Before you pack it in for the evening, take a few minutes to go over what you've seen. If you've been out an hour or so, you'll notice that the sky has moved a bit around the north celestial pole. This, of course, is due to the rotation of the Earth. Also, the next time you go out, be sure to find the objects you already know to reinforce your knowledge of them. Then press on into "unexplored territory."

It might seem odd to mention clothing in a book on the sky, but there's method to my madness: a clear sky is cold, really, really cold. In fact, the sky is so cold that it'll suck the heat right out of your body, especially considering that you're just standing there peering at the sky, rather than walking around keeping yourself warm. So, wearing one more layer of clothes than you would normally wear is a really good idea. And a nice, warm hat is always a good thing to wear. Having a Thermos of coffee, tea, or soup will also help you ward off the chill of the night. Finally, the *piece de resistance* is a PBJ sandwich!

I also recommend a specific piece of furniture for use in viewing the sky. It's the venerable (and cheap) folding recliner. (You know. The one that goes "click-click-click" as you unfold it.) The reason for using such a pedestrian device is not just pure comfort, although I'm all for that. It's just that a person who is relaxed will see more, longer. There's a down side, though. If you get too comfortable, you might just fall asleep. I did that once, at my club's observatory in the Lockwood Valley of southern California. I woke up several hours later with a nice crust of frost on my mustache!

You might also want to keep a journal to help you remember what you've seen. I've included one at the end of this book to get you started.

A day of exploring is behind you. Supper is over. Now it's time to explore those dark, spectacular national park skies.

Where to Find Additional Help

✦ ✦ ✦ ✦ ✦ ✦ ✦ ✦ ✦ ✦ ✦ ✦ ✦

Many books include tables or diagrams that tell you things like the phases of the Moon, times of sunrise and sunset for any day of the year, and where the bright planets may be found in the sky on a particular date. There's no room for that in this lean book. But it might surprise you to find that the weather pages of most newspapers provide a wealth of astronomical information. You just have to read the proverbial fine print.

While visiting a national park, you'll likely find that information on the times of sunrise, sunset, moonrise, and moonset, along with the phase of the Moon, will be posted on some bulletin board, somewhere in the park. The trick is to find that board.

Your visit to a park will certainly be enhanced by attending an evening interpretive program given by a ranger or volunteer. The majority of the national parks have such programs, and the numbers are growing. (And, of course, if you need to know something basic like "which way is north," the person presenting the program will be happy to tell you that, and a lot more.)

THE SKY FROM HOME Once you return home from your visit to a park, I hope you'll continue observing the night sky. You'll likely find that your local skies are brighter at night than those you found during your visit to a park. The members of your local astronomy club will be able to tell you where to go to reach dark(er) skies in your local area. They'll also invite you to join their club, and I certainly suggest that you take them up on it. You'll learn a lot about doing astronomy, and you'll probably meet a lot of nice, interesting folks as well.

You'll likely want to have a way of finding out what's happening in the sky and when it's happening. There's a list of publications, software, and websites inside the back cover of this book that should help. Also, the members of your hometown astronomy club will be able to advise you on sources of astronomy information.

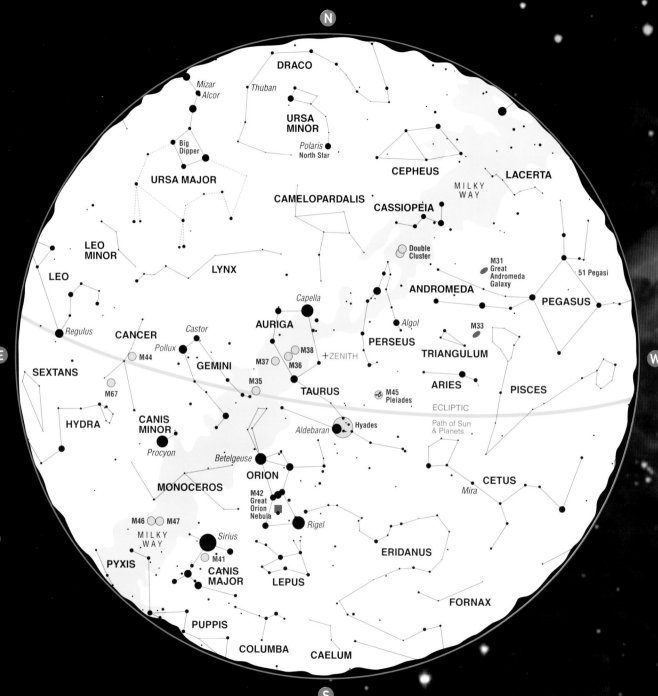

USE THIS CHART

JANUARY 1 AT 11:20 PM
JANUARY 15 AT 10:20 PM
FEBRUARY 1 AT 9:20 PM
FEBRUARY 15 AT 8:20 PM
MARCH 1 AT 7:20 PM

01 – 02

N

DRACO

Mizar
Alcor

Thuban

URSA
MINOR

Big
Dipper

Polaris
North Star

CEPHEUS

LACERTA

URSA MAJOR

MILKY
WAY

Double
Cluster

CASSIOPEIA

CAMELOPARDALIS

LEO
MINOR

M31
Great
Andromeda
Galaxy

51 Pegasi

LYNX

ANDROMEDA

PEGASUS

LEO

Capella

Regulus

CANCER

Castor

AURIGA

M38

PERSEUS

Algol

M33

TRIANGULUM

ARIES

PISCES

Pollux

+ ZENITH

M44

M37
M36

CANIS
MINOR

SEXTANS

GEMINI

M35

TAURUS

M45
Pleiades

ECLIPTIC
Path of Sun
& Planets

M67

HYDRA

Hyades

CANIS
MINOR

Aldebaran

Procyon

Betelgeuse

ORION

CETUS

Mira

MONOCEROS

M42
Great
Orion
Nebula

Rigel

ERIDANUS

M46   M47

MILKY
WAY

Sirius

PYXIS

M41

LEPUS

FORNAX

CANIS
MAJOR

PUPPIS

COLUMBA

CAELUM

S

E

W

STAR MAGNITUDE

● BRIGHTEST ★ MAG –1 TO 0
● BRIGHT ★ MAG 1 TO 2
● AVERAGE ★ MAG 2 TO 3
• FAINT ★ MAG 4 TO 5

OBJECTS TO VIEW

● CLUSTERS OF STARS
✦ GLOBULAR CLUSTER
■ NEBULA
○ PLANETARY NEBULA
▱ GALAXY

ALL-SKY MAPS

The following six *all-sky maps* will help you navigate your way through the nighttime sky. Please don't assume that, just because an object isn't listed in the narrative, it isn't worth viewing. Also, don't expect to see everything I've described during your first night out. Some of the objects I've described are quite challenging. I included them to make sure you don't get bored!

The Glorious Winter Milky Way

On winter nights the air is usually low in humidity, so the stars seem to jump out at us. We're looking away from the center of our Galaxy into the Orion Arm, a little detour in the main spiral arm known as the Sagittarius Arm. Outward from us is the Perseus Arm. Since we're in the outer portion of the Orion Arm, there's not a lot of dust to obscure our view. That's why all those stars are so bright.

If you stand facing south and look about a third of the way up from the southern horizon, you'll find Sirius, a blazing blue-white star. It's so bright because it's close, only about eight light-years away. It won't take much imagination to see that Sirius is the heart of a dog, Canis Major, looking up at its master. If you pan slowly east away from Sirius with your binoculars, you should see a wealth of galactic clusters, some of which I've identified on the map. Another fine cluster, M41, is about 5 degrees south of Sirius.

Canis Major's master is the anchor of the winter sky, Orion, the Hunter. Almost everyone who's ever learned the sky easily remembers the three stars that make up Orion's belt. Hanging down below his belt is his sword, another group of three (fainter) stars. You can likely see that the middle of these three is fuzzy. That's the Great Orion Nebula, M42, a bubble of gas and dust that's about 1,500 light-years distant, and about 50 light-years across. It's a nice-looking object in your binoculars, glowing a soft green, but a telescope shows it in all its glory, complete with a quadruple star known as the Trapezium embedded in it. This nebula is the finest we can see here in North America. I never pass up a chance to view it, despite the fact that I've seen it, literally, thousands of times!

Orion also features two great stars: His right shoulder is a bright orange-red star known as Betelgeuse ("armpit of the Great One" in Arabic) and Rigel marking his right knee. Far to the left of Betelgeuse is the pure-white Procyon, and just above that star are twin stars, Castor and Pollux. You can see them near the zenith (the "top of the sky") where they define the head of Gemini, the Twins. If you pan down near the feet of the Twins, you'll find M35, a galactic cluster that's the 35th on Messier's list of great DSOs (Deep Sky Objects).

If you move your view toward the west, you'll find a huge pentagon of stars anchored by the yellow-orange star Capella. Panning through this area of the winter Milky Way will net you many galactic clusters, including M36, M37, and M38.

Just west of the zenith, you'll find a gorgeous small "dipper" of stars known as the Pleiades. Just next to the Pleiades are the Hyades, a V-shaped group of stars with a bright orange star, Aldebaran, at the top right of the V. The Pleiades are a group of hot, young stars that all formed out of the same nebula, but there's no hydrogen left to form new stars, just dust, which forms a dim nebula that can be seen on dry, dark (unpolluted) nights. The Hyades are about 450 light-years away, but Aldebaran is only half as far. It's just part of the Hyades from our point of view. Finally, the Hyades and the Pleiades are part of a large, fanciful constellation known as Taurus, the Bull.

The Great Orion Nebula, one of our galaxy's great "stellar nurseries" in which multitudes of stars are forming. Embedded deep within this nebula is the magnificent quadruple star system known as the Trapezium.

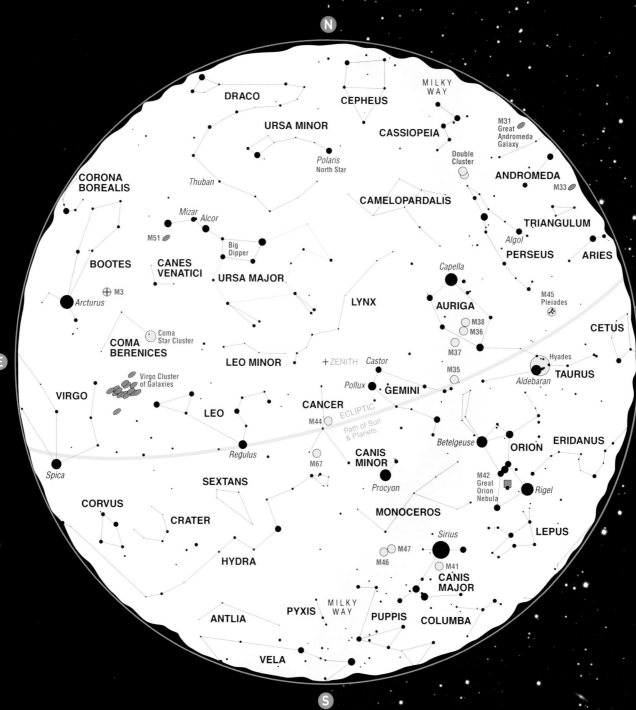

03 – 04

N

DRACO

CEPHEUS

MILKY WAY

URSA MINOR

CASSIOPEIA

M31 Great Andromeda Galaxy

Polaris North Star

Double Cluster

ANDROMEDA

M33

Thuban

CAMELOPARDALIS

TRIANGULUM

CORONA BOREALIS

Mizar Alcor

Algol

PERSEUS

ARIES

M51

Big Dipper

BOOTES

CANES VENATICI

Capella

URSA MAJOR

M45 Pleiades

CETUS

Arcturus

M3

LYNX

AURIGA

M38
M36

COMA BERENICES

Coma Star Cluster

M37

LEO MINOR

ZENITH

Castor

M35

Hyades

TAURUS

Aldebaran

E

Virgo Cluster of Galaxies

Pollux

GEMINI

W

VIRGO

LEO

CANCER

ECLIPTIC
Path of Sun & Planets

Betelgeuse

ORION

ERIDANUS

M44

Regulus

M67

CANIS MINOR

M42 Great Orion Nebula

Rigel

Spica

SEXTANS

Procyon

MONOCEROS

LEPUS

CORVUS

CRATER

Sirius

HYDRA

M47

M46

M41

CANIS MAJOR

PYXIS

MILKY WAY

PUPPIS

COLUMBA

ANTLIA

VELA

S

STAR MAGNITUDE

● BRIGHTEST ★ MAG -1 TO 0
● BRIGHT ★ MAG 1 TO 2
● AVERAGE ★ MAG 2 TO 3
• FAINT ★ MAG 4 TO 5

OBJECTS TO VIEW

● CLUSTERS OF STARS
✦ GLOBULAR CLUSTER
■ NEBULA
○ PLANETARY NEBULA
✦ GALAXY

A Lion, a "Little Cloud," and Galaxies – Lots of Galaxies!

This close-up view of the Beehive Cluster (M44) as seen through a powerful telescope. With the naked eye or binoculars you'll see a blur, or "Little Cloud," as the ancients called it.

After the glamour and glitter of January/February skies, those of March/April are a bit tamer. All the bright winter stars line the western horizon. But there's still a lot to see. We'll start by facing south and noticing that there aren't a lot of bright objects in view. That's because we're now mostly looking away from the Orion Arm of our Galaxy.

But near the zenith we find a bright white star, Regulus, that forms the bottom of a group of stars shaped like a big hook. Just to the east, or left, of that group you'll see a squat triangle of stars. If you put them together, you get a pretty fair lion. The hook is his forepaws and mane, and the triangle defines his haunches. Leo, as he's called, isn't quite up to "MGM" quality, but it takes little imagination to see him up there. As you can see, the ecliptic passes very close to Regulus. This means that the Moon, which is always within 5 degrees of the ecliptic, often passes between us and Regulus.

About halfway from Regulus to the twin stars, Castor and Pollux to the west, you'll notice a large faint "fuzzy object." The ancients called this group the Little Cloud, because they couldn't resolve it into stars. The reason, of course, is that the telescope hadn't yet been invented. You can resolve M44, what we now call The Beehive, with your binoculars. It's a galactic cluster, and when you first see it, you'll probably understand how it got its name. It's also a decent test of how dark a night you have. If you can't see the "little cloud" with just your naked eyes, you have either a lot of clouds closer to you or light-polluted skies.

If you turn around and face north, you'll find the Big Dipper, Ursa Major, in its "dump the stars" mode. Just below it is the Little Dipper. (If you can trace the entire Little Dipper, you have a fairly dark night.) Polaris, or the Pole Star, lies at the end of the handle of the Little Dipper. Because it's so close to the north celestial pole, it doesn't appear to move from hour to hour. Look one star in from the end of the Big Dipper's handle to find a visual double star, Alcor and Mizar.

If you view this pair in a decent small telescope at medium power, you'll find that Alcor is itself a double.

If you look toward the southeast and near the horizon, you'll find a bright, blue-white star, Spica, flanked by a kite-shaped asterism to its right. The "kite" is Corvus, the Crow, which is a bit hard to see. But Spica anchors Virgo, the "reclining virgin." Seeing such a figure there is a test of your imagination!

Between Corvus and the Big Dipper lie two different clusters of galaxies, the Virgo Cluster, and the Coma Cluster. I'll not direct you to view any of them, because viewing them really isn't within the scope of this book. Visiting a star party where large telescopes will be set up on a spring night will allow you a tour of these galaxies.

If you look about a third of the way up from the eastern horizon, you'll spot Arcturus, a bright yellow-red star that's the harbinger of the summer stars to follow. Moving your gaze another third of the way to the zenith will take you to Coma Berenices, the only constellation in the sky that's not the conventional connect-the-dots variety. It's a loose galactic cluster of stars that's supposed to represent the golden hair of Berenice, the Queen of Ptolemy, an ancient king of Egypt. Her hair was allegedly shorn to celebrate the winning of a great battle. The hair was apparently lost by the court astrologer who, to save his skin, claimed it had been placed in the sky to honor the victory.

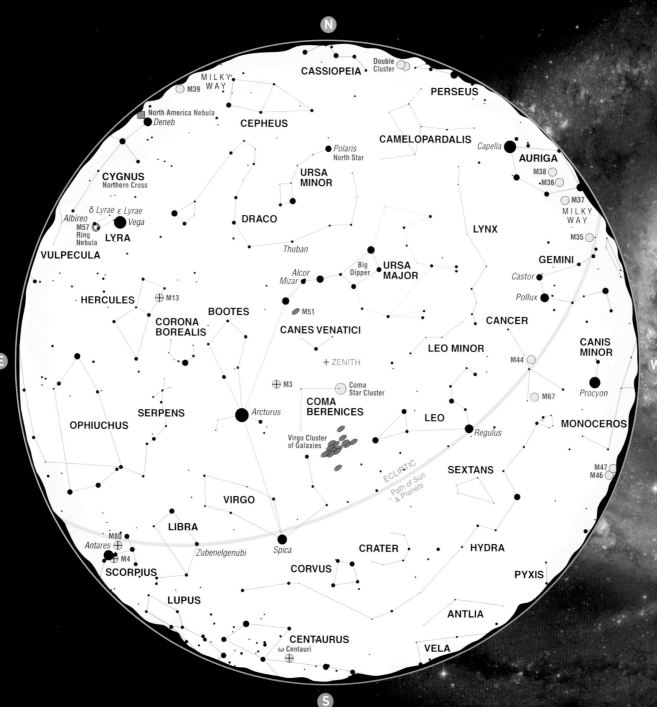

05 – 06

STAR MAGNITUDE

● BRIGHTEST ★ MAG -1 TO 0
● BRIGHT ★ MAG 1 TO 2
● AVERAGE ★ MAG 2 TO 3
• FAINT ★ MAG 4 TO 5

OBJECTS TO VIEW

● CLUSTERS OF STARS
⊕ GLOBULAR CLUSTER
■ NEBULA
○ PLANETARY NEBULA
⬭ GALAXY

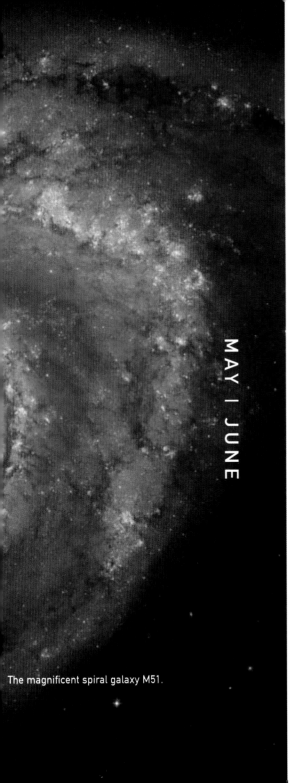

The magnificent spiral galaxy M51.

A Herdsman, *the* Globular Cluster, and a Wonderful Spiral Galaxy

MAY/JUNE SKIES

We start our tour of the May/June sky with a herdsman. Looking due south and near the zenith, you'll find a bright, reddish-yellow star, Arcturus. We also identified it in the narrative for March skies. As the chart shows, Arcturus is the anchor star of the constellation Boötes. Immediately to his right you'll find Coma Berenices, followed by Leo heading toward the horizon. Just to the left, or east, of Boötes, you'll find a lovely half-circle of stars that are well described as Corona Borealis, or the Northern Crown.

There's a silly memory aid that will help you remember how to navigate this part of the sky. Find the Big Dipper, and note how its handle appears to curve toward Arcturus. If you continue that approximate curve about the same distance, you come to Spica. The aid is "spiraling down to Spica" from the Dipper. (I told you it was silly.)

The constellation Scorpius may be found on the southeastern horizon, with the star Antares at the heart of the scorpion. You'll be able to see its tail much better in the summer months. Leading the scorpion across the southern sky is Libra, the Scales. The brightest star in that nondescript constellation, Zubenelgenubi, is actually a very nice double star that's easy to split with binoculars.

Between Libra and the southern horizon are a lot of fairly bright stars. They make up Centaurus, the Centaur, which is no more easy to recognize than Virgo. But, lurking among those stars, just to the west of due south, is an amazing globular cluster known as omega Centauri. It's easily the closest, biggest, and brightest of the globulars, but it's so far south that you need to be living in the southern tier of states in the United States to see it. Omega is about the size of the full Moon, and contains something like a million stars, so it's easy to view in binoculars. Make sure you see omega Centauri if you travel south, and try to get a look at it in a telescope. You won't regret it!

There are some beautiful sights in the east, but you can read about them in the narrative for July, so I'll use this space to tell you about one of the few galaxies that's worth finding in binoculars or a small telescope. It's M51, which you'll find just about 5 degrees southwest of the end of the Big Dipper's handle. In binoculars, M51 is basically an elongated smudge. Its story is better than your view of it. M51 is a spiral galaxy very much like our own, and we're looking at it from directly above or below its pole. There the similarity ends. Just beyond it, another galaxy is making a close pass and is ripping one of the spiral arms off M51 (see photo at left). The other galaxy isn't doing much damage, though. Space is so vast, even in a dense galaxy, that astronomers calculate that it's about even money that only two stars will collide due to this event. A 6-inch telescope will reveal M51 as just a mottled disk of light with a smaller, denser companion. Larger telescopes show what I described here.

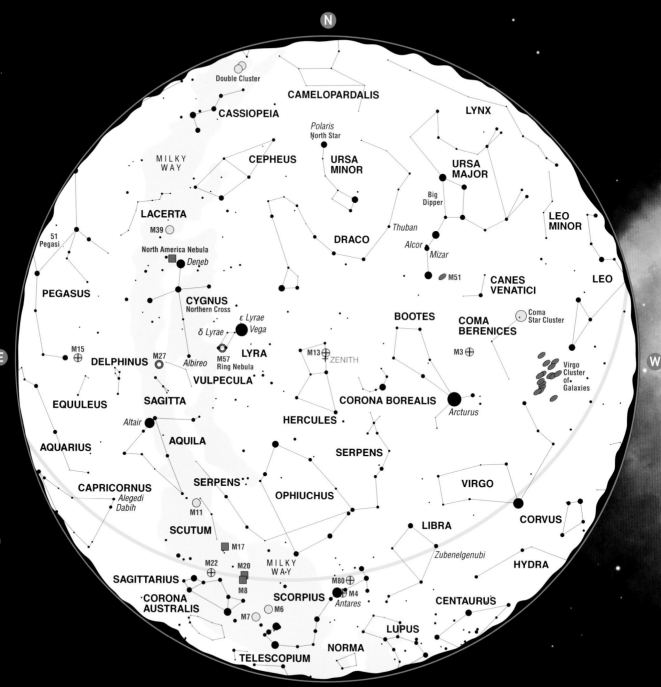

07 - 08

N

Double Cluster

CAMELOPARDALIS

CASSIOPEIA

LYNX

MILKY WAY

Polaris
North Star

CEPHEUS

URSA MINOR

URSA MAJOR

LACERTA

M39

Big Dipper

LEO MINOR

51 Pegasi

North America Nebula

Deneb

DRACO

Thuban

Alcor

Mizar

LEO

PEGASUS

M51

CANES VENATICI

CYGNUS
Northern Cross

ε Lyrae
Vega

BOOTES

COMA BERENICES

Coma Star Cluster

M15

δ Lyrae

DELPHINUS

M27

M57
Ring Nebula

LYRA

M13

ZENITH

M3

Albireo

VULPECULA

Virgo Cluster of Galaxies

E

EQUULEUS

SAGITTA

Altair

CORONA BOREALIS

Arcturus

AQUILA

HERCULES

W

AQUARIUS

SERPENS

VIRGO

CAPRICORNUS

Alegedi
Dabih

SERPENS

OPHIUCHUS

M11

CORVUS

SCUTUM

LIBRA

Zubenelgenubi

HYDRA

M17

MILKY WAY

M22

M20

M8

SAGITTARIUS

SCORPIUS

M80

CENTAURUS

CORONA AUSTRALIS

M7

M6

M4

Antares

LUPUS

TELESCOPIUM

NORMA

S

STAR MAGNITUDE

● BRIGHTEST ★ MAG -1 TO 0
● BRIGHT ★ MAG 1 TO 2
● AVERAGE ★ MAG 2 TO 3
• FAINT ★ MAG 4 TO 5

OBJECTS TO VIEW

● CLUSTERS OF STARS
✪ GLOBULAR CLUSTER
■ NEBULA
○ PLANETARY NEBULA
⬭ GALAXY

The Glorious Summer Milky Way

In July and August we can look into the heart of our Milky Way Galaxy. It stretches from the southern horizon clear across the sky to the horizon just a bit east of north. Space doesn't permit giving you a detailed description of all you can see along the Milky Way, but you'll be rewarded handsomely by just strolling up and down that milky band with your binoculars.

If you face south and look toward the zenith, you'll find the blue-white star Vega, which is part of the constellation Lyra, the Lyre. The Lyre is defined by the little parallelogram of stars just southeast of Vega. Vega is the brightest star in the northern half of the sky. It appears so bright because it's only about 25 light-years away, and it's about 58 times as bright as the Sun. There are two nice double stars in Lyra that you can split in your binoculars: δ Lyra, and ε Lyra. Delta is a nice pair. The brighter of the two is white, while the dimmer is orange-red, especially in contrast with the white member of the pair. Epsilon Lyra is a gorgeous white-white pair. But, when viewed through a medium-sized telescope, each star of the pair is revealed to be a double star itself.

Just west of Lyra you'll find a Hercules, the Strongman, which would be about as boring as a Steve Reeves movie on cable except for the marvelous globular cluster M13. M13 is one of the showpiece globular clusters in the northern sky. It's about 25,000 light-years distant and may contain more than half a million stars. Sharp-eyed observers can see M13 without optical aid on a dark night. Can you? (Don't fail to see this cluster in as large a telescope as you can find.)

From Vega to the southern horizon we can proceed along the Milky Way toward the galactic center. On the way, note bright Altair, flanked by two stars of almost equal brilliance. Altair is a star that rotates so fast that it's about twice as wide as it is thick. It's also the eye of Aquila, the Eagle, one of those constellations that actually could be what is claimed for it. Just below Aquila you'll find Scutum, the Shield, which is one of those constellations that just squeaked onto the list in the seventeenth century to honor a victorious Polish king's battle shield, of all things. Scutum is unrecognizable and unremarkable, except for the glorious galactic cluster M11. It's an object that reminds everyone of a handful of jewels. M11 is a glorious binocular object.

But the *piece de resistance* in July's sky is the Scorpius-Sagittarius region, an amazing collection of deep sky objects for your viewing pleasure. You can see two galactic clusters, M6 and M7, just off the tail of the scorpion. Can you see them without your binoculars? If you place those two clusters at the bottom edge of your binocular field, you'll find the galactic center just above the top edge of the field. But don't expect to actually see it. There are about 35,000 light-years of gas and dust obscuring our view of it.

There are many nebulas in the region, but M8, M20, and M17 stand out. The first two are known as the Lagoon Nebula and the Trifid Nebula. Both names denote the fact that there are lanes of dust obscuring part of each nebula. M17 is called the Swan, Omega, or Check-mark Nebula. When you first see M17 with a good telescope, you'll know why. But they're so bright that you can see them all without your binoculars, and they're fine views in binocs.

Scanning the region in binoculars will give you great views of bright nebulas and clusters. But don't forget the dark nebulas. They're all over the place, and their subtle beauty is worth the view just for themselves. My favorite lies between the spout of the "Teapot" asterism of Sagittarius and Antares, but you'll see more as you work your way up the Milky Way from there. You might have a different favorite dark nebula. Speaking of Antares, it's a red giant star that's late in its evolutionary life. Its name means "Rival of Mars" in Greek. Its red color is the reason for that name. Its color also indicates that it's very cool. Antares is also known to be huge. It would easily contain our entire inner Solar System, right out to Mars!

Finally, the Scorpius-Sagittarius region is home to many globular clusters. M4 may be found just west of Antares, while M22 may be found just above the lid of the Teapot. There are a lot more, but these two are the best of the lot.

The Helix Nebula (NGC 7293), one of the closest of all planetary nebulas. This class of object is called a planetary nebula because early observers found that it looked like the disk of a ghostly planet.

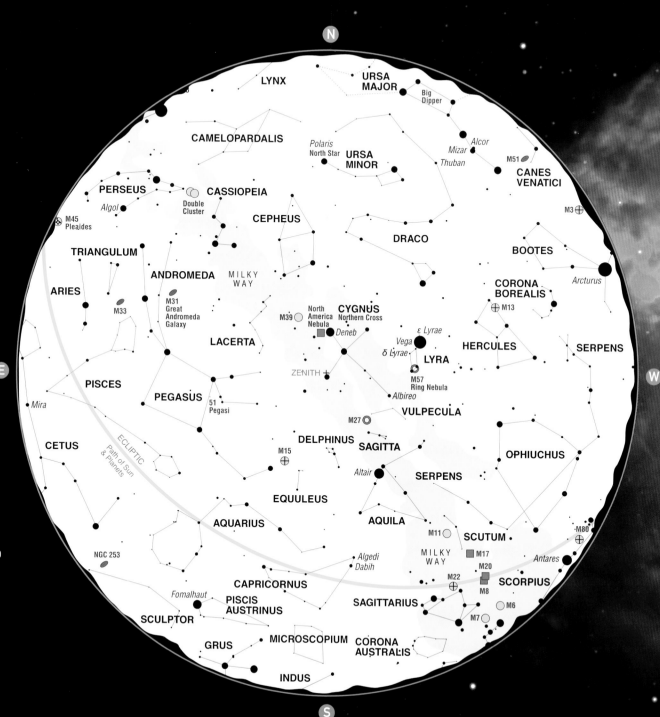

USE THIS CHART

SEPTEMBER 1 AT 11:20 PM
SEPTEMBER 15 AT 10:20 PM
OCTOBER 1 AT 9:20 PM
OCTOBER 15 AT 8:20 PM
NOVEMBER 1 AT 7:20 PM

N

LYNX

URSA MAJOR

Big Dipper

CAMELOPARDALIS

Polaris North Star

URSA MINOR

Mizar
Alcor

Thuban

M51

CANES VENATICI

PERSEUS

CASSIOPEIA

CEPHEUS

DRACO

M3

BOOTES

Algol

Double Cluster

M45 Pleaides

TRIANGULUM

ANDROMEDA

MILKY WAY

CORONA BOREALIS

Arcturus

ARIES

M31 Great Andromeda Galaxy

M33

M39

North America Nebula

CYGNUS
Northern Cross

ε Lyrae

M13

HERCULES

SERPENS

E

LACERTA

Deneb

Vega
δ Lyrae

LYRA

PISCES

PEGASUS

51 Pegasi

ZENITH

M57
Ring Nebula

Albireo

W

Mira

VULPECULA

CETUS

DELPHINUS

M27

M15

SAGITTA

OPHIUCHUS

Altair

SERPENS

EQUULEUS

AQUILA

AQUARIUS

M11

SCUTUM

M80

STAR MAGNITUDE

● BRIGHTEST ★ MAG -1 TO 0
● BRIGHT ★ MAG 1 TO 2
● AVERAGE ★ MAG 2 TO 3
• FAINT ★ MAG 4 TO 5

NGC 253

Algedi
Dabih

MILKY WAY

M17

M20
M8

Antares

CAPRICORNUS

M22

SCORPIUS

Fomalhaut

PISCIS AUSTRINUS

M6

SCULPTOR

SAGITTARIUS

M7

OBJECTS TO VIEW

● CLUSTERS OF STARS
✪ GLOBULAR CLUSTER
■ NEBULA
○ PLANETARY NEBULA
▱ GALAXY

GRUS

MICROSCOPIUM

CORONA AUSTRALIS

INDUS

S

A Great Square, the North America Nebula, and a Dumbbell

The wonderful Dumbbell or Butterfly Nebula (M27) in the constellation Vulpecula. This is one of the closest and largest planetary nebulas in the sky.

After the summer's view of the gaudy region near the galactic center, the sky in early fall might seem a bit tame. But it's well worth your time to view. As usual, begin by facing south. You'll see the bright star Fomalhaut about a quarter of the way from the southern horizon to the zenith.

One thing you might also notice is that Fomalhaut is in a region that's devoid of other bright stars. This chance situation leads to Fomalhaut being used as the star to which interplanetary spacecraft are directed to find and then align themselves. The reason is that there's less chance of the simple-minded robot device being confused by other bright stars if there are none near the target.

Immediately to the right of Fomalhaut is Capricornus, which vaguely resembles the sea-goat it's supposed to be. Capricornus features two nice double stars for you to split with your binoculars. Both α and β Capriconi are widely separated. Alpha is of almost equal magnitude, and you can split it with your naked eye, while beta's companion is three magnitudes dimmer than the primary. Above Fomalhaut is Aquarius, complete with a jar in which to carry the water. Moving up toward the zenith, you'll notice an enormous square of stars just east of the zenith. It's the Great Square of Pegasus.

Pegasus is supposed to be a winged horse. But the square is what we more modern observers see. The star in the northeast corner of the square actually lies in the constellation Andromeda (see page 27). The star 51 Pegasi was the first sun around which astronomers found solid evidence of a planet. To our view, though, it's just another nondescript star. The globular cluster M15, however, is hardly nondescript. It's a real beauty that you'll find about a width of the square west of the square.

If you swing around and face west, you'll see a nice Latin cross west of the zenith. It's the Northern Cross, which is actually part of Cygnus, the Swan. As a swan, it's flying toward the horizon. Its nose, or the bottom of the cross, is defined by Albireo, one of the most beautiful double stars in the sky. Even viewing that star with binoculars reveals a wide blue and gold pair.

Cygnus is home to some nice dark nebulas and arguably the most difficult object to see that I'll describe in this book. It's the North America Nebula (NGC 7000), a huge cloud of gas and dust that resembles the North American continent. What actually determines the shape we see is dust between us and the nebula. I've included the North America Nebula as an example of a subtle object you can see on a night that's truly dark. It can be seen without optical aid but is much easier to locate with binoculars. There are many dark nebulas in Cygnus worth viewing, along with several galactic clusters. M29, near the "criss" of the "cross" is the brightest of these.

Just south and east of Albireo you'll find M27, the closest and brightest planetary nebula in the sky. It's so big and bright that it's often mistaken for a comet by neophyte sky observers. (When I first found M27 through a telescope at age 12, I was sure I had discovered my first comet. More careful perusal of my star atlas deflated my mood!) In a telescope M27 resembles a weightlifter's dumbbell, so it's called the Dumbbell Nebula. Others call it the Butterfly. In binoculars, it's a bright oblong patch of misty light. In a large telescope, M27 is truly glorious. Don't miss it.

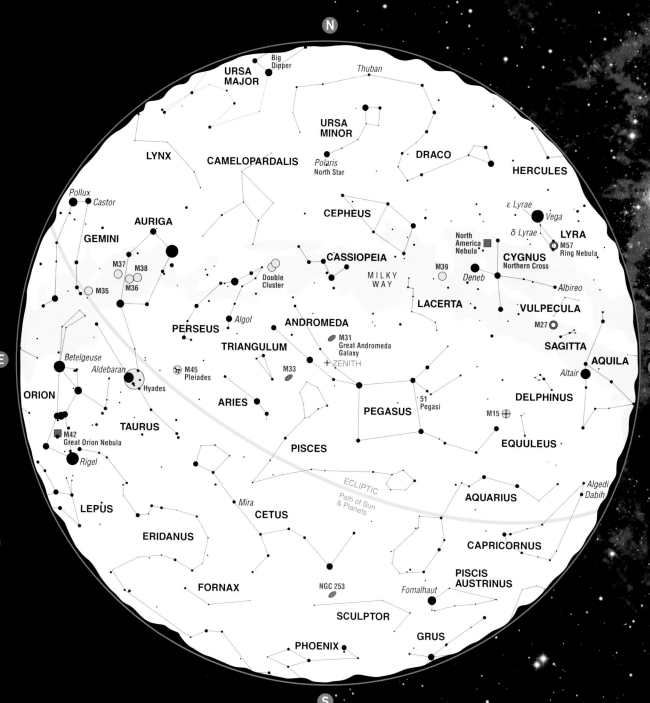

USE THIS CHART

NOVEMBER 1 AT 11:20 PM
NOVEMBER 15 AT 10:20 PM
DECEMBER 1 AT 9:20 PM
DECEMBER 15 AT 8:20 PM
JANUARY 1 AT 7:20 PM
JANUARY 15 AT 6:20 PM

STAR MAGNITUDE

⬤ BRIGHTEST ★ MAG -1 TO 0
● BRIGHT ★ MAG 1 TO 2
• AVERAGE ★ MAG 2 TO 3
· FAINT ★ MAG 4 TO 5

OBJECTS TO VIEW

● CLUSTERS OF STARS
✦ GLOBULAR CLUSTER
■ NEBULA
○ PLANETARY NEBULA
⬗ GALAXY

N

S

E

W

URSA MAJOR
Big Dipper
Thuban
URSA MINOR
DRACO
HERCULES
LYNX
CAMELOPARDALIS
Polaris North Star
CEPHEUS
ε Lyrae
Vega
Pollux
Castor
AURIGA
δ Lyrae
LYRA
GEMINI
M37
M38
M36
M35
Double Cluster
CASSIOPEIA
North America Nebula
M57 Ring Nebula
M39
CYGNUS Northern Cross
Deneb
MILKY WAY
Albireo
LACERTA
VULPECULA
PERSEUS
Algol
ANDROMEDA
M27
SAGITTA
TRIANGULUM
M31 Great Andromeda Galaxy
AQUILA
Betelgeuse
ZENITH
Altair
Aldebaran
M45 Pleiades
M33
DELPHINUS
Hyades
ORION
ARIES
PEGASUS
51 Pegasi
M15
TAURUS
EQUULEUS
M42 Great Orion Nebula
PISCES
Rigel
LEPUS
Mira
CETUS
ECLIPTIC Path of Sun & Planets
AQUARIUS
Algedi
Dabih
ERIDANUS
CAPRICORNUS
FORNAX
NGC 253
PISCIS AUSTRINUS
Fomalhaut
SCULPTOR
GRUS
PHOENIX

The Great Andromeda Galaxy, Mira (the Wonderful), Algol (the Demon)

NOVEMBER | DECEMBER

The Triangulum Galaxy (M33), part of the Local Group of galaxies, which includes the Andromeda Galaxy (M31) and our own galaxy, the Milky Way.

In late fall, we see a transition from a group of stars that are relatively inconspicuous to another group of gaudy stars embedded in the Milky Way. But the very fact that there aren't as many stars means that we're looking out of our galaxy into the deep space beyond.

If you face west and find the Great Square of Pegasus, you'll notice a graceful arc of stars attached to the top star in the square. Just to the right of the second star in the arc you should see a "faint fuzzy." You may have to use averted vision to find it.

That faint fuzzy is one of the closer galaxies in our own Local Group of galaxies. It's the Great Andromeda Galaxy, another spiral galaxy like ours, only a bit bigger. The Andromeda Galaxy, or M31, is about 2.1 million light-years away, which is really close for a galaxy. In binoculars you should be able to see it as an elongated ellipse as big as 4 degrees across. In a modest telescope it shows a very bright core and its two satellite galaxies. A large telescope reveals the subtle lanes of dust between the spiral arms and the fact that the core is a very pale yellow (due to the stars in the core being very old).

South of the arc of stars that defines Andromeda, you'll see Triangulum, the (what else?) Triangle. The lovely galaxy M33 is in Triangulum and is really the only object of note in that constellation. M33 is a very subtle, not very organized spiral that's about 2.7 million light-years away, also in the Local Group. M33 is interesting because it has a nebula in it that's so big and bright that you can see it in a six-inch telescope despite its great distance. If you can see M33 without optical aid, you have one of the nights of your life.

Smack-dab in the middle of the area of dim stars between Orion and Aquarius is a constellation known as Cetus, the (mostly invisible) Whale. You'll want to find your way around Cetus, because it features a wonderful object. It's known as Mira. It's a variable star that fades from a bright magnitude 2 to as dim as magnitude 10, all in the space of about 331 days.

In Arabic, Mira means "The Wonderful," as the ancient astronomers would have called anything that faded to well below naked-eye visibility and then brightened again. (Mira does this because it's become unstable at the end of its life and is pulsating. When it's big and cool, it puts out most of its light in the infrared spectrum, which we can't see. When it's small and hot, it radiates more of its light in the red end of the visible spectrum. In a telescope it looks red.)

Just west of the mouth of the Whale you'll find an elongated patch of light that's about the size of the full Moon. It's the galaxy NGC253. It's an easy object to spot in binoculars, one of the few galaxies about which we can say that. If you can get a look at NGC253 in a large telescope, you'll be rewarded with a view of a vast spiral galaxy, complete with lanes of dust between the spiral arms.

If you spin around to face north, you'll notice the Big Dipper grazing the northern horizon. Just above Polaris, you'll find Cassiopeia and a group of stars in the shape of a slightly squashed "M," which some folks see as an upside-down "W." Cassiopeia is the Queen of Ethiopia, and she's also the mother-in-law of Perseus, the Hero, the group of stars to her right. (Cepheus, the King is just below and to the left of Cassiopeia.) Between Cassiopeia and Perseus lies the lovely Double Cluster, a galactic cluster that can be seen with the naked eye but is glorious in binoculars or a telescope.

Perseus is also the home of Algol, a star that varies in brightness because it's really a double star system. One star eclipses the other every 2.87 days, causing us to see a dip in its brightness from 2.2 magnitude to 3.5 magnitude. Because of this, the Arab astronomers called Algol "the Demon."

Earth's Moon

The image of the full moon you see to the right makes a nice, basic moon map. Because it was taken at full moon, the craters don't stand out in sharp relief. Of course, that's because the Sun is shining mostly "straight down" onto the Moon's surface. But this image does show the larger features of the Moon that you can see with the naked eye or with binoculars.

Looking at the Moon as the phases progress is magic, because there's a new slice of the surface available each night, and that slice is seen at high contrast, because that's where the Sun has just risen, and the shadows are very long. After full Moon, you'll have to stay up later and later to see it, but each slice will be illuminated from the opposite direction as it was during the first half of the *lunation* (period from one new Moon to the next) so it'll look a bit different.

I'll not provide you with a crater-by-crater description of the Moon's surface. However, here are some general notes that I hope will enhance your lunar viewing experience.

O The craters are very old and are believed to have been formed by asteroids crashing into the young lunar surface more than 4.2 billion years ago. One of the more prominent craters, Copernicus, is about 60 miles across and 2$\frac{1}{5}$ miles deep. It's also one of the younger craters.

O The mountains you see on the Moon aren't mountains such as we have here on Earth—they weren't pushed up by tectonic plates colliding with each other. Rather, they're the edges of huge, ancient craters that formed extremely early in the life of the Moon. Other asteroids slammed into the Moon later, causing lava to flow over some edges of these huge craters, leaving the rest of the crater intact as a short mountain range. You'll notice that the Apennine Mountains are just a bit in the shape of a crescent. In your mind's eye, continue that crescent to make a circle. The original crater must have been a doozy!

O The maria are relatively new areas of the Moon that have been flooded by lava from the last major asteroid strikes that formed the larger craters. The word *maria* is Latin for "seas." Before the telescope was invented, these smooth, darker areas were thought to be the oceans of the Moon, because the human eye can't resolve the smaller craters that populate the maria.

O Aside from craters and mountains and maria, you can see rays on the Moon with your binoculars, especially near full Moon. These are broad, light-colored lines that streak away from several craters. One ray that starts at the young crater Tycho continues a distance of nearly 2,000 miles across the Moon's disk as we see it! What are they? Well, the short answer is that they're splash marks where molten lava landed when an asteroid hit the Moon. As proof, I point out that rays radiate straight away from craters.

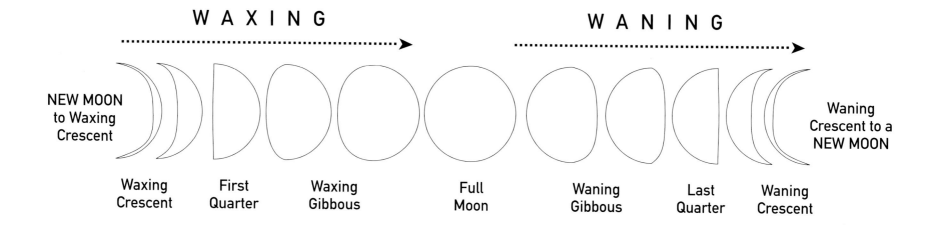

WAXING

NEW MOON to Waxing Crescent

Waxing Crescent

First Quarter

Waxing Gibbous

Full Moon

WANING

Waning Gibbous

Last Quarter

Waning Crescent

Waning Crescent to a NEW MOON

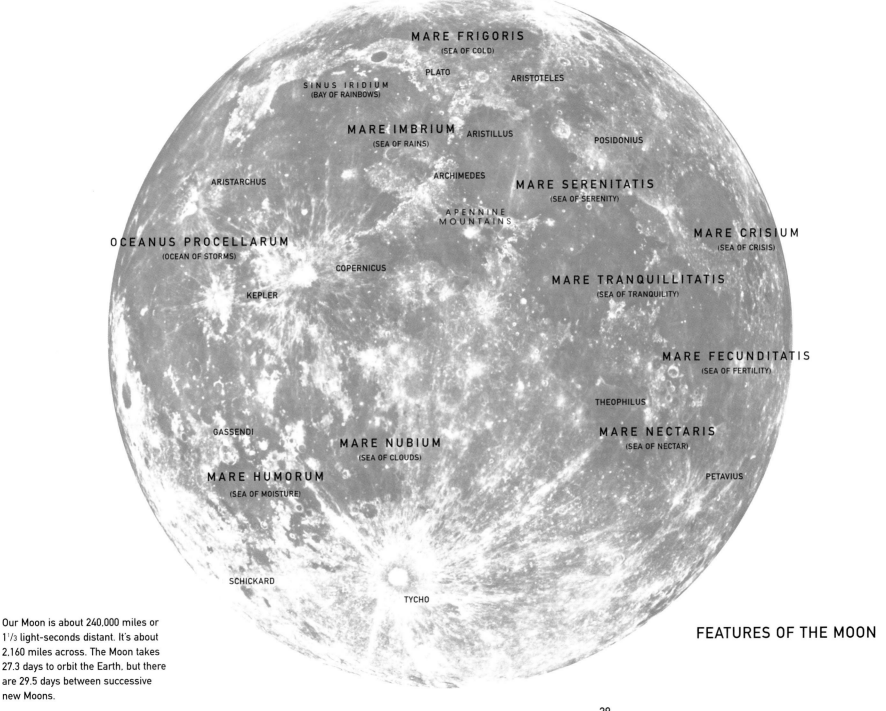

MARE FRIGORIS
(SEA OF COLD)

PLATO

ARISTOTELES

SINUS IRIDIUM
(BAY OF RAINBOWS)

MARE IMBRIUM
(SEA OF RAINS)

ARISTILLUS

POSIDONIUS

ARISTARCHUS

ARCHIMEDES

MARE SERENITATIS
(SEA OF SERENITY)

APENNINE
MOUNTAINS

MARE CRISIUM
(SEA OF CRISIS)

OCEANUS PROCELLARUM
(OCEAN OF STORMS)

COPERNICUS

MARE TRANQUILLITATIS
(SEA OF TRANQUILITY)

KEPLER

MARE FECUNDITATIS
(SEA OF FERTILITY)

THEOPHILUS

GASSENDI

MARE NUBIUM
(SEA OF CLOUDS)

MARE NECTARIS
(SEA OF NECTAR)

MARE HUMORUM
(SEA OF MOISTURE)

PETAVIUS

SCHICKARD

TYCHO

Our Moon is about 240,000 miles or 1 1/3 light-seconds distant. It's about 2,160 miles across. The Moon takes 27.3 days to orbit the Earth, but there are 29.5 days between successive new Moons.

FEATURES OF THE MOON

So You Like Dark Skies, Do You? Here's How to Keep Them.

* * * * * * * * * * * *

The idea behind writing this book was to provide you with a simple, compact, inexpensive introduction to what you can see under a dark sky. I hope you'll agree that the previous pages have succeeded in that goal.

As I mentioned in the introduction, I have an ulterior motive. It's to get you hooked on looking at the sky, so hooked that you'll share my outrage that our dark skies are disappearing. This last section will provide a brief guide to things you can do to reverse the trend toward skies that are increasingly polluted with stray light.

Power Hungry? The evolution of our modern society in the twentieth century was powered by the twin revolutions of electricity and the automobile.

Although both were developed in the final years of the nineteenth and the first few years of the twentieth century, electricity and the automobile didn't really come into their own until the economic expansion driven by World War II.

If people could get in their cars and go places after working all day, they expected that there would be lighted outdoor recreation facilities available to them when they got there. When they went to the new shopping centers, they expected well-lit parking lots waiting for them. Also, the revolution in communications meant that the average American was much more aware of crime. That led to an increased awareness of the "need" for security lighting.

It simply became commonplace for us to expect that wherever we went, day or night, there would be a well-lit, secure environment. It didn't matter that well-lit didn't always mean "secure." We were conditioned to believe that it did.

The table on page 32 illustrates just how much the use of electricity has expanded in the United States since the end of World War II. But the satellite image below vividly shows that the amount of light we're blasting up into the sky has even outpaced the increase in use of electricity.

Can We Afford It? No, we can't afford it. The supply of fossil fuels (oil, gas, and coal) isn't being renewed, and other sources of power have various disadvantages space

This map of world light pollution was produced by the University of Padova in Italy. It shows the amazing amount of light shining up and being scattered by atmospheric molecules, water vapor, clouds, and dust into the glare we see in our night sky.

won't permit me to discuss. From just an economic standpoint, we really must radically reduce the amount of light we waste.

From a medical and social standpoint, we need to change our ways, as well. There are numerous scientific studies that suggest that interrupting our *circadian rhythm* of alternating light and dark contributes to a variety of human illnesses. It's doing the same thing to our wildlife, who don't have the capability to just install dark curtains in their bedrooms. And socially, we're losing our connection to the stars under which our forebears evolved.

What to Do? We've become conditioned to not having a dark night. Here's an example from my personal experience:

I moved to Cornville, a rural community south of Sedona, Arizona, in late 1994. Shortly after I arrived, I had occasion to go to Sedona one evening to see a friend. I found myself driving along Highway 89A, the main drag. I was having a bit of trouble reading a couple of street signs, and thought to myself, "Jeez! It's really dark in this town. I can't read the street signs. They really oughta get some street lights in here."

Then, of course, I mentally slapped myself for thinking such an outrageous thought. I've done astronomy since I was 10 and always decried the spread of light pollution wherever I've lived. But, on this night, I wanted *more light!* If I can fall for that, anyone can.

So, for starters, those of us who are now concerned about light pollution must ensure that *we're* not polluting. We need to look around our own homes and businesses to see what contributions we're making to light pollution. This takes several forms:

We need to reduce the overall amount of light we use. I noticed that I had a 60-watt bulb in my porch light. I changed it to a 15-watt bulb. That's small potatoes, but I've also noticed how absurdly bright the lights at my local mini-mart are. Could every other fluorescent tube be removed to reduce the amount of light

Bad lighting

Good lighting

it's putting out?

Regardless of the amount of light we're generating, *we really must stop shining any light directly into the sky.* The images above on the right and on the next page illustrate properly designed light fixtures. Their fundamental features are that they cut light off so it can't shine above the horizon. This means that more of the light that's being produced is shining where it should, and less is being wasted. (Here's a really important point: If less light is being shone into the sky, a lower-wattage bulb will provide the same level of light on the ground than when the fixture was

wasting light.) But there's a more important result: Since most outdoor surfaces are poor reflectors of light, a lot less of the light being generated ends up in the sky.

So, if half of the light from a 100-watt bulb shines into the sky, there's nothing to stop it from polluting our dark sky. But if all the light generated by that same bulb is directed at the ground, and only 10 percent is reflected into the sky, we've reduced the light pollution from that bulb by 80 percent. And if we decide to replace the 100-watt bulb with a 50-watt bulb, the light pollution is reduced by 90 percent, and we're using only half the power we were before.

Amount of Electric Power Generated in the US

YEAR	AMOUNT OF POWER	POPULATION
1952	0.404 million-million KwH	157.5 million
1962	0.858 million-million KwH	186.5 million
1972	1.753 million-million KwH	209.9 million
1982	2.244 million-million KwH	231.7 million
1992	3.084 million-million KwH	255.0 million
2002	3.839 million-million KwH	290.0 million

In the 50-year period detailed above, our electric power use increased almost 10 times, while our population "only" doubled. Unfortunately, a lot of that electric power has gone straight up into the sky as stray light.

A row of well-designed streetlights shine their light only down onto the pavement below. Since the pavement reflects only 10 to15 percent of the light that hits it, little light finds its way into the night sky.

Getting Your Neighbors and the Community Involved

This pair of pictures illustrates just how much of the night sky is obliterated when ordinary lights are allowed to shine up into the sky. Violet represents the least amount of light pollution, white the most. Notice how much darker Pinnacles National Monument is than Santa Monica Mountains National Recreation Area, in Los Angeles.

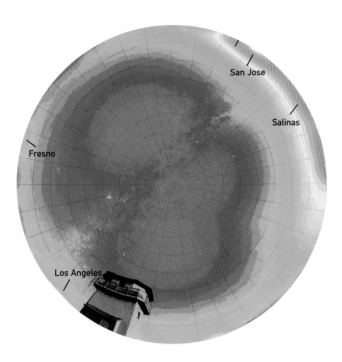

Pinnacles National Monument

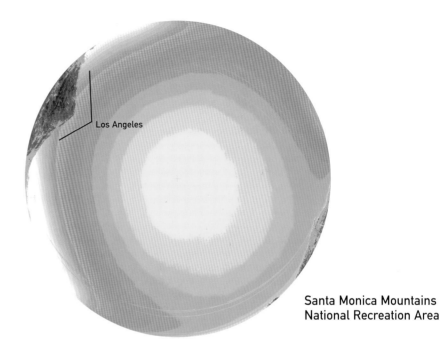

Santa Monica Mountains National Recreation Area

No one really likes whining at his neighbor about a problem, be it a dog barking, loud music blaring, or a really bright light blasting all over the neighborhood. I've found that the easiest way to make my neighbors aware of the light pollution they're causing is to invite them over to look through my telescope. They quickly get the picture as they try to squint at something through the eyepiece because of the searchlight next to their garage. If you don't have a telescope, just invite your neighbors over to view the sky through your binoculars. You can also astound and amaze your neighbors with your newfound knowledge of the constellations!

I've also found that showing a local businessperson how she can both save money and reduce how much light her place of business shines into the sky is often met with acceptance, if not downright enthusiasm. (The key is to make suggestions in a non-confrontational manner.) Also, if you participate in drafting clear, con-cise local light-pollution abatement ordinances in your city or town, you can have a positive influence on reducing light pollution. A member of my local club has done that in both his home town of Clarkdale, Arizona, and in the neighboring city of Cottonwood.

If you're serious about being part of the effort to reverse the growth of light pollution, you'll want to join the International Dark-Sky Association. It's based in Tucson, Arizona, but is truly international in scope. The IDA has an enormous number of free resources available at its website: www.ida.org. I hope you'll check it out.

What's Being Done in the National Parks? In the 1990s, the National Park Service realized that light pollution was beginning to impact the dark skies in the parks here in the western United States. A Night Sky Team was formed among NPS personnel throughout the region. All the members serve on the team in addi-tion to their regular work, so it's truly a labor of love.

To define the light pollution in the parks in the West, the NPS Night Sky Team enlisted the aid of the International Dark Sky Association, the US Naval Observatory, and a group of astronomers at the University of Padova in Italy. This international group came up with a digital camera that is capable of rapidly taking 114 images of the night sky and storing them in a computer. A computer program then stitches all 114 into one seamless image of the brightness of the sky. The images you see above were made with this camera.

By the end of 2005, the NPS expects to have imaged the night sky in 44 parks in the western United States. This database of images will allow the managers of the various parks to work with their own staffs and with their surrounding communities to identify sources of light pollution and then to reduce that pollution.

A Final Note

* * * * * * * * * * * * * * *

As you've taken this dark sky tour, you've learned how much there is to see in the sky with just your eyes or with a simple pair of binoculars. You've also found how much your view can be limited by light that's strayed into the sky. It won't be easy, but we can get our dark skies back. It will take the efforts of a lot of folks just like you, all working in their communities. And there's one big advantage to solving light pollution.

Once you turn off a light, or direct it away from the sky, there's no residual pollution to clean up....Just a nice, dark sky!

Resources

* * * * * * * * * * * * * *

WEBSITES

www.skyandtelescope.com
www.astronomy.com
www.stardate.org
science.nasa.gov
hubblesite.org
www.darksky.org
www.heavens-above.com

MAGAZINES

Sky & Telescope
Astronomy
SkyNews

BOOKS

Terence Dickinson. *Nightwatch: A Practical Guide to Viewing the Universe.* Kingston, Ontario: Firefly Books, 1998.

Guy Consolmagno and Dan M. Davis. *Turn Left at Orion: A Hundred Night Sky Objects to See in a Small Telescope--and How to Find Them.* New York: Cambridge University Press, 2000.

Rick Shaffer. *Your Guide to the Sky.* New York: McGraw-Hill, 1999.

ASTRONOMY SOFTWARE

Starry Night (www.starrynight.com)
TheSky (www.bisque.com)

Copyright © 2006 by Richard Shaffer
Published by Western National Parks Association

The net proceeds from WNPA publications support educational and research programs in the national parks. Receive a free Western National Parks Association catalog. Email: info@wnpa.org or visit www.wnpa.org

ISBN-10 1-58369-062-X
ISBN-13 978-1-58369-062-8

Written by Rick Shaffer
Edited by Steve Phillips
Designed by Melanie Doherty Design, San Francisco
Sky charts by Carolyn Randall
Photography — Cover: Frank Zullo; Page 1 and back cover: NASA, ESA, and S. Beckwith (STScI and the HUDF Team); Page 2: Richard Payne; Page 4: Frank Zullo; Page 5: NASA/ESA and The Hubble Heritage Team (STScI/AURA); Page 6: Rick Shaffer; Page 7 (left): ESA, NASA and Martino Romaniello (European Southern Observatory, Germany); Page 7 (right): Remi Lacasse; Page 9: Frank Zullo; Page 11: NASA/STScI; Page 13: NASA, ESA and E. Karkoschka (University of Arizona); Pages 14-15: Frank Zullo; Pages 16-17: Remi Lacasse; Pages 18-19: NOAO/AURA/NSF; Pages 20-21: NASA/ESA and The Hubble Heritage Team (ScI/AURA); Pages 22-23: NASA, NOAO, ESA, the Hubble Helix Nebula Team, M. Meixner (STScI), and T.A. Rector (NRAO); Pages 24-25: G. Jacoby, WIYN/NOAO/NSF; Pages 26-27: T.A. Rector (NRAO/AUI/NSF and NOAO/AURA/NSF) and M. Hanna (NOAO/AURA/NSF); Page 29: UC Regents/Lick Observatory; Page 30: Craig Mayhew and Robert Simmon, NASA/GSFC; Page 31: John Coons, Flagstaff Dark Skies Coalition; Page 32: Frank Zullo; Page 33: National Park Service.

Printing by Imago
Printed in Thailand

Nighttime Sky Journal

* * * * * * * * * * * * *

Save Your Discoveries! Keeping a journal is a great way to "remember" your nighttime observations and discoveries. Jotting down what you see (and even what you don't!) will not only accelerate your learning process but will also save those great dark sky park experiences.

So what should your journal look like? I've included the following forms as a starting point. By the time you've filled out the sheets, you'll probably have a pretty good idea of what form your next journal will take. Meanwhile, this journal is here for you to record your observations as you start out.

Merely recording the name of the objects you've viewed will probably be enough for you as you start out. But a more elaborate record would include a drawing. Most folks find a pencil a good tool because they can smear it to draw "fuzzy objects." And most draw objects with black for white and white for black. A lot less lead and time get consumed that way. (Of course, if you're drawing the planets, you'll want to use some sort of color medium.)

Finally, by keeping a record of your nighttime observations at various parks, you'll be able to compare one site to another. Where were the nighttime skies especially good for observation? What parks or other observation locations suffer most from stray light from urban areas? You may find that dark skies are a lot more important than you ever imagined!

OBSERVING RECORD FOR:

_____ | _____
date | *time (from-to)*

PARK OR OTHER SITE:

_____

DARKNESS/TRANSPARENCY:

Poor 1 2 3 4 5 *Dark*

WHAT I OBSERVED:

_____
_____
_____
_____
_____
_____
_____
_____
_____
_____
_____
_____
_____
_____
_____
_____
_____

OBSERVING RECORD FOR:

_____ | _____
date | *time (from-to)*

PARK OR OTHER SITE:

_____

DARKNESS/TRANSPARENCY:

Poor 1 2 3 4 5 *Dark*

WHAT I OBSERVED:

_____
_____
_____
_____
_____
_____
_____
_____
_____
_____
_____
_____
_____
_____
_____
_____
_____

Nighttime Sky Journal

* * * * * * * * * * * * *

OBSERVING RECORD FOR:

date　　　*time (from-to)*

PARK OR OTHER SITE:

DARKNESS/TRANSPARENCY:

Poor　1　2　3　4　5　Dark

WHAT I OBSERVED:

OBSERVING RECORD FOR:

date　　　*time (from-to)*

PARK OR OTHER SITE:

DARKNESS/TRANSPARENCY:

Poor　1　2　3　4　5　Dark

WHAT I OBSERVED:

OBSERVING RECORD FOR:

date　　　*time (from-to)*

PARK OR OTHER SITE:

DARKNESS/TRANSPARENCY:

Poor　1　2　3　4　5　Dark

WHAT I OBSERVED:

Nighttime Sky Journal

✴ ✴ ✴ ✴ ✴ ✴ ✴ ✴ ✴ ✴ ✴ ✴

OBSERVING RECORD FOR:

_____|_____
date   *time (from-to)*

PARK OR OTHER SITE:

_____

DARKNESS/TRANSPARENCY:

    Poor   1   2   3   4   5   Dark

WHAT I OBSERVED:

OBSERVING RECORD FOR:

_____|_____
date   *time (from-to)*

PARK OR OTHER SITE:

_____

DARKNESS/TRANSPARENCY:

    Poor   1   2   3   4   5   Dark

WHAT I OBSERVED:

OBSERVING RECORD FOR:

_____|_____
date   *time (from-to)*

PARK OR OTHER SITE:

_____

DARKNESS/TRANSPARENCY:

    Poor   1   2   3   4   5   Dark

WHAT I OBSERVED:

Nighttime Sky Journal

* * * * * * * * * * * * *

OBSERVING RECORD FOR:

_____|_____
       date   *time (from-to)*

PARK OR OTHER SITE:

_____

DARKNESS/TRANSPARENCY:

     Poor   *1*   *2*   *3*   *4*   *5*   *Dark*

WHAT I OBSERVED:

OBSERVING RECORD FOR:

_____|_____
       date   *time (from-to)*

PARK OR OTHER SITE:

_____

DARKNESS/TRANSPARENCY:

     Poor   *1*   *2*   *3*   *4*   *5*   *Dark*

WHAT I OBSERVED:

OBSERVING RECORD FOR:

_____|_____
       date   *time (from-to)*

PARK OR OTHER SITE:

_____

DARKNESS/TRANSPARENCY:

     Poor   *1*   *2*   *3*   *4*   *5*   *Dark*

WHAT I OBSERVED:

Nighttime Sky Journal

✳ ✳ ✳ ✳ ✳ ✳ ✳ ✳ ✳ ✳ ✳ ✳

OBSERVING RECORD FOR:

_____ | _____
date | *time (from-to)*

PARK OR OTHER SITE:

_____

DARKNESS/TRANSPARENCY:

    Poor   1   2   3   4   5   Dark

WHAT I OBSERVED:

OBSERVING RECORD FOR:

_____ | _____
date | *time (from-to)*

PARK OR OTHER SITE:

_____

DARKNESS/TRANSPARENCY:

    Poor   1   2   3   4   5   Dark

WHAT I OBSERVED:

OBSERVING RECORD FOR:

_____ | _____
date | *time (from-to)*

PARK OR OTHER SITE:

_____

DARKNESS/TRANSPARENCY:

    Poor   1   2   3   4   5   Dark

WHAT I OBSERVED:

Nighttime Sky Journal

∗ ∗ ∗ ∗ ∗ ∗ ∗ ∗ ∗ ∗ ∗ ∗ ∗

OBSERVING RECORD FOR:

date　　　*time (from-to)*

PARK OR OTHER SITE:

DARKNESS/TRANSPARENCY:

Poor　1　2　3　4　5　*Dark*

WHAT I OBSERVED:

OBSERVING RECORD FOR:

date　　　*time (from-to)*

PARK OR OTHER SITE:

DARKNESS/TRANSPARENCY:

Poor　1　2　3　4　5　*Dark*

WHAT I OBSERVED:

OBSERVING RECORD FOR:

date　　　*time (from-to)*

PARK OR OTHER SITE:

DARKNESS/TRANSPARENCY:

Poor　1　2　3　4　5　*Dark*

WHAT I OBSERVED: